Black Lawrence Press
www.blacklawrence.com

Executive Editor and Art Director: Colleen Ryor
Managing Editor: Diane Goettel
Book Design: Steven Seighman

Copyright © 2009 Matthew Gavin Frank

All rights reserved. Except for brief quotations in critical articles or reviews, no part of this book may be reproduced in any manner without prior written permission from the publisher:

Black Lawrence Press
8405 Bay Parkway C8
Brooklyn, N.Y. 11214
U.S.A.

Poems in this work have originally appeared in *Bat City Review, Cairn, Crazyhorse, Epoch, Hayden's Ferry Review, The Journal, Meridian, The New Republic, Ninth Letter, North American Review, Pleiades, Rosebud, 6x6,* and *Verse Daily.*

The long poem, *Aardvark,* originally appeared as a chapbook of the same title, published by West Town Press, 2007.

Cover art: "Stump" by Jen Burton

Published 2009 by Black Lawrence Press, an imprint of Dzanc Books

First edition 2009

Printed in the United States

SAGITTARIUS AGITPROP

poems

Matthew Gavin Frank

Black Lawrence Press
New York

CONTENTS

ONE

Zodiac	13
Elegy for the Eunuch Sagittarius	14
Parts of a Feather	15
Sagittarius at Dusk	17
Communion	18
My Infant Daughter	19
Begging	20
Gathering after the Spleen	23
More Trouble on the St. Lawrence	24
Because of Citrus	26
Saucer	27
Sagittarius, Sleeping	28
Mirrors	30
The Dressmaker's Dummy	32
Ars Poetica	34
For Avery	35
For Linda	36

TWO

Yehoshua's Star	41
Buying a Gun on the Internet, or, I'm Mad at My Family	43
Sagittarius Nocturne	45
Shabbat	46
Sagittarius Does Syracuse	47
Memorial Day	48
Elegy for the Whitefish	49
Buffalo	50
Sprouts	51
The Upstairs Cow	52
Frida Kahlo	54
1962	55
Ossification	57

THREE

Aardvark	61

For Louisa Johanna:

Clean up your room.

Love like a ponderous trained bear
Danced upright at our slightest will

—*Guillaume Apollinaire*

Oh daddy, be proud of your planet
Oh mommy, be proud of your son

—*Mick Jagger*

ONE

Zodiac

Is that a muskrat or a wheelbarrow
pushing itself across Sixteenth?

The little blonde girl with the tree-frog
balloon points from a pink sleeve

and shouts, *Muskrat!* Her mother,
in a green neoprene kerchief (Coiffure

d'Avignon is just around the corner),
jerks her pink arm into dislocation.

The popping sound arrests me, as does
the silver dollar push of bone that jumps

from the girl's collar. I've never been good
at these things; at deciding what they really

are. I have trouble distinguishing
between hornets and horseflies.

On my back, I can't tell if that's your finger
or your breath.

Elegy for the Eunuch Sagittarius

A lampshade of hummingbird tongues hums
its light. It is light enough.

Three kilometers away, Henry prepares
his tweezers with a butane lighter.

(Nothing erotic
can save you now).

On the lighter's sequined flank, a cowgirl in pantaloons
prepares to bite through a stallion's ear,

the air in her mouth, bare,
weightless as a jellyfish. In the sugarwater trap,

a pandemonium of wings. The animal
like a liver in Henry's hand.

The word you want to say still hides
under a ten-gallon hat,

rubbing salve on its cock.

Parts of a Feather

The superstitious geometry of the rock dove rests
between its first and fifth rib. And you

rest between it. It's easy
to call you a disease. Better: a heart or rain

or our dinner plates, last night draped in the leavings
of cherry. *Of course*, you say, *my hands*

are the skeletons of everything with wings, hiding
art in their armpits. You say, a feather stripped

of barbs is bone. I say, Don't get me started
on Venice. Too many chicken frescoes laying

their ossuary, Stravinsky tied with a piano string.
He plucks a music like yolk. Good for you. Bad

for you. Bursting with fat. That was the honeymoon,
whole storms going on in there. Your mother

wouldn't have put up with this. She was too big
a fan of Picasso: *an idea is never as interesting*

as its ear. So, here we stand, naked as iron,
the puddle for the hail. A marriage license

makes a lousy umbrella and, even worse,
a wonderful canal. But still you convince me,

gravity is only weather, and electricity,
the closing of the beak. Let's stand

outside in it, watch the planes revise Andromeda.
We'll make it. I assure you. Tonight, you play

the worm. Strange how, to fly, the dead bird
needs the hurricane.

Sagittarius at Dusk

In the sand, the crab
turns over, shoots its white belly
to the teenage girl, jogging in yellow
shorts. She thinks it's a dime

but is too wary of the fat-legged
fisherman with the blue-and-white lure
to pick it up, find out
it's a crab.

The fisherman just became a grandfather
at forty-one, holds in his heart
a scrap of metal the size
of a dime. The purple he sees

is not real, the egret dies eating.
The strangest things keep us alive at dusk.
From this bench, I can see the power plant,
but not the tired people inside

murmuring their small stories
in between small sparks.

Communion

There is something of sleep
that is the hushing of a bird's feathers

being shuffled by other birds.
The day travels by train, bridging

both lobes, each errand shuffled
and repeated like a deck of cards.

The cards know the importance
of silence and repeated words:

Each king, each queen, lying back-
to-front with the jacks and numbers, lit

with indecency, must recall
the supermarket, the blue soap

on sale, the hole in the shoulder
of the postman's shirt. There is something

of the mouth that calls to these,
in the uniform of sleep, as a bird

collecting a flock, an ant, who
when threatened with a fall,

discovers that it can spin a web
like a spider.

My Infant Daughter

My infant daughter is talking to whales.
She forgets Montreal, who
once screamed, *to the ocean!*
On the river, the muskrats stop
eating at dusk.

After she unravels her feet, her tiny elbow in the blowhole,
she hears the coal in the stove
coming to rest on these peninsulas of heat
and only one mother. It must be hers.

My aunt, as a child, always,
heaped into the linen closet by her brother, whispered
Lock me in with a pitchfork handle, the one
daddy never used.

He believed the river ended
in Arizona.

Now, my mother doesn't remember any of us.
Not with this sort of health care.

It's so easy to forget, spreading her eyes like nickel, blind
to fire and to the grandchildren. Inside the fire is the kayak
the whale will have to use.

Begging

She asks her daughter not to mind
the rain. "It's safe," she tells her.

But the daughter, fresh from fields
of tractor

wait:

fields of bedroom, from the flocks
of Black Guillemot, clings to her inshore

waters, her small group
of auks. Their desire to kill

is somehow collaborative, the pigeon-
sized want to redden their mouths

to sow-bait

wait:

redden their mouths
to flowers with the meat of the crabs.

With tongues like eels

wait:

> With tongues like Least Brook
> Lampreys, they lick the tulips

wait:

> petals from their lips. Still
> with the taste of Canada, still with
>
> the taste of Miss—

wait:

> Still with the taste of Canada, she will
> fall South, trying, even through
>
> the monsoons, to hold her neck high.
> Her arms will go tributary.

wait:

> Her limbs will go river. She will go
> door-to-door, try selling you
>
> her hairbrush
> for two dollars or a bag of almonds

wait:

> a can
> of soup.

If she fails, she will return
to bedrooms strewn with rung peacocks.

wait:

a kitchen strewn with her mother's
dead cats. Plugging her nose, she will dive

again into the arctic blankets of water, remember
her kill, and surface, spitting mouthfuls of flowers.

wait:

mouthfuls
of Mississippi.

Gathering After the Spleen

His mother lost her spleen, poor thing.
She'd confused the hot and cold sides
of the faucet. The doctor told him: *dirty
laundry for a week, and chili from the can.*
At home, while she bit into the dishtowel
and sweat through her sheets, he gathered
three of his friends. That night, the moon
was only the moon.

One of the boys had been experimenting
with electricity: light
bulbs and lampshades, butter-churners
and paint. "It can be done."
Under only the moon, spinning night's
fabric into vinyl, the boys
crab-walked through a hole
in the hospital's fence. They found
the garage, the team of ambulances sleeping
like gorillas on their feet. Beyond the last
ambulance—the largest of the bunch,
the hairiest of chests—they found it, wooden
and missing

a handlebar. Here, they passed
their first cigarette, gently letting
the air from the tires
of the cart that their pain rides in.

More Trouble on the St. Lawrence

Force-fed, like coffee through a filter, bruises
on your knees, you claim

ownership: sleep, money, the orange recliner.
You sit on a colonial couple

hauling oranges with horses, a plank of wood
with wheels attached. You rock

them into repetition, swallow your English
muffin with strawberry jam.

Prometheus told me to tell you, "Go
fuck yourself." I can't

believe you're taking classes again. What
would your mother

say about this? *There's more to being Mayan
than reading about dreams.*

Stringing time together with electrical
pioneering. When you

shore up in your sleep, a horse bucks. When
you bite your lip, fall

into oranges. Who can tell you that your dream
is only the squawking

of a thrift store chair, a diploma cast
in mohair and pressed

with an iron. Like a calf's tongue. (We paid
thirty dollars for this whole thing).

How many times do you need to see your name
calligraphic? How many frames

can one word take? I should tell you: you press
your elbows to your ribs,

a whole hurricane, like a loaf of bread, unspinning
into bone. In the morning,

when the light is like this, I think of hospitals.

Because of Citrus

The body is a parcel, shamelessly spilling
its oranges. Blood, navel,

sweet. Paper-wrapped and unzested, pith
left to tickle the crack of one's ass.

Because of citrus, we can cringe. Because
the juice, we cry. Like the body, drinking

is obvious. But this is not the body.
Not really. The emptied peel we leave

is only the whale to something smaller,
trying, as we all do, to make love

to another small, same thing.

Saucer

Here is the saucer upon which my father's head
pools like coffee. He's beyond medication.
The hummingbirds have overtaken him, bricking
his smile with sugarcubes. When he speaks to me,
his tongue taps his teeth, a teaspoon gently ringing
the hour against the lip of his favorite mug. The one
I brought back from Alaska. The one with three
moose: mother, father, child. A cow, a bull, a twig
pulled from a nest, cracked with eggshell and cream.
I adjust his napkin. I bring him his coffee. In the bathroom,
a few hairs from his old beard still cling to the sink.

Sagittarius, Sleeping

Under the blanket is not
the fable we expect, morality divined
from the blossoms
in the mattress.

You will dare to say
snowflake, then
orchid aloud
before the bathroom mirror, or
the reflection of the mirror in the wings
of the mosquito.

This is where they build
their family, all the actual things
that ask to be remembered
as fictions: the walk through

the vacant lot where there will
soon be houses, kissing her there
the sky orange
or purple, scarred
with telephone wire and Starling,
the field mice ecstatic
in the raveled work
of milkweed, thinking about
the first bite into your ankles,
a diagram of the most thrilled
ingredient in blood, broken
skin, then thinking against it.
Sex

and the waking very early
in an apartment outside
a city in the desert
and the light there, carving
a cheekbone into the red wall, painted
over, pleading.

Mirrors

The mosquito wrinkles against the glass, bites
at its own reflection. My sister wonders
if it sees itself as the bear trapped in its blue

image, the bite of rusted aluminum at its ankles,
thick as quicksand. My sister begins a story
about handcuffs and brass bedposts, then

remembers I'm her brother. I glance
at her wrists, looking for scars. Someone
should tell us not to think so much about

the mosquito, not to clap our hands on its flight,
igniting the small firecracker of God-knows-
whose blood onto our palms, not to close

our fronds over the wrists of another.
Sometimes, someone should tell us, the wrists
will maneuver a harmonica over a bearded

man's lips. Sometimes, the sound of a harmonica
played by one's father is gargantuan, explosive
as a firecracker, especially if one's mother

has locked herself into the bedroom again,
threatening to burn all of the paperbacks.
He wouldn't care, but he needs to know

the endings. It is only the beginnings that matter
to her. Soon, they will put down their instruments,
find the time to make love six times before the last

few pages. A brother will hold his sister's hand
at their closed door, as I may hold my sister's,
wishing it was a book of matches. The air

will be heavy with trying rain, and we
will ask of it, before it falls: *Tell us our names*
will be carried on in the saliva of mosquitoes,

our holes will be mended with simple needle
and thread. And tell us also, that our parents
will never die.

The Dressmaker's Dummy

She stands

as if nobly eviscerated, rib-
cage inflated as a balloon, a balloon's

skeleton, a mold, a blueprint, this headless,
limbless torso graces the wall

above our dinner table. Who could have
predicted her thirty-three-dollar rescue

from among
bicycles, pillowless sofas, pants

with undone pleats? Who could have predicted
my wife's unpredictable taste that thrift

store morning in mid-July, when her sense
of female kinship was never more deadly

nor delicious? The lack of blood alone
suggested its age. "An antique?" she would ask

the tattooed woman at the register, an adornment
of skulls, masks, birds of prey darting

from ankle to the rolled rim of denim short,
"Over fifty years old?" The answer

was the squalling of the register, shrieking
toward the total as an eagle toward a salmon,

state's tax, sales tax, life's, and death's surely
included. We take her home. She lies

on her side in the trunk. She is scarily
dependable. A small nail later, a delicate

hammering later, she hangs, always
hangs as we twirl our fettuccine, as we

undress and love and argue, as we fork
the meat of all dinners

into our excited mouths.

Ars Poetica

The grass is hot, the air
a brush dripping paint,
and an adolescent blue hog
noses what it thinks
is a potato sack.

A Sitka deer died here yesterday,
its belly full of stew: hemlock needles,
laurel leaves, carrot,
potato. Yesterday,

the boy who shot the deer
climbed a flagpole in front
of the closed middle school, fell
and broke his arm. The clover,
left its mark on his neck.
I don't know why he did this,
but I can guess.

In the solarium, his mother sneezes
blood into a handkerchief.
This is cherry season. The boy dreams
of cherries,

the hog roots under the deer,
the day comes to a boil.
I don't think

I'm supposed to see this.
I think we must be fearful.

For Avery

For all the loving, love. Like a hanger
with blue wool on it. Like a blue sheep

mad with sickness, at the moon
for turning colors. You bear the burden

of reward. It weighs about four pounds.

Sometimes, the world hides itself behind
the patio furniture in the way-back

of the garage, the big-armed chairs you will,
one summer, improperly stain, puddling

the patio purple like old murder.

For all the new, renew. Like the library
book on birdfeeders you will desperately

want to save a dollar on. Like a recipe
for Harissa, or the child who hates

Harissa, and because of this, loves you.

Not because of this: the stains at your collar,
the spit-up formula smell ringing

your neck with premature lemon. That special
way you hang your shirts, carefully, to mask

their heartlessness.

For all the hearts in this apartment, sing
circus songs to a newborn.

For Linda

Her hands so full of husband,
it looks like she's wearing gloves,
my aunt said, six Thanksgivings ago.
She would never

say *love* over a turkey.

Linda, I know.
You never open the windows in your apartment,
your curtains, lace carved into rock.

If I understood the language, I'm sure
they'd tell a story about the Starling
picking dead bees from the sill,

how they know all about
Emily Dickinson's ghost, and the largest
mansion in Kentucky. I know.

The iron smell of his sweat
on the olive green pillowcase,
thin as a veil, I know,

wonder if the milk, spoiling in the fridge,
has a sound. If it can commune with the last day
you cried over something stupid
or the ballpoint pen that signed the letter.

I imagine, as you must have, the big
hand of that man, plunging the red
military stamp into its corner, starstruck.

From across your living room, it can be lipstick,
Marilyn Monroe. This all must be
an old movie, played into an empty mansion.

I want to tell you: I want to be
in the mind of the Starling, where my brother's body
is just something else
to land on.

TWO

Yehoshua's Star

We are displaced even by the stars,
ben Zakkai says, a tortoise bone oar

tilting in his hands. Federico
doesn't know what to make of this,

has never before shared a rowboat
with a beardless Rabbi. He clears

his throat and reaches for the bladder
of *pulque.* The night is cold. The night

shows too much of itself without a window
to trim its edges. The stars push

quinoa in black broth, hardening
to chestnuts over one ocean or another.

Without a lid, they are overdone.
What we need, Zakkai says, *is another*

Cousteau, someone to explain
why the stars are the product

of sea crabs, the bioluminescent algae
reflecting from their shells, pushed

41

upward by water. Federico dreams
the colors of their claws, musters

the *pulque.* "Is this why Mars is red?"
The ocean pitches like a pumpkin

falling down stairs, seeds collecting
at Andromeda's middle. Zakkai

corrects a jellyfish with the oar,
holds it to Federico. Its intestines spin

white into an orchid, draw the stars
like bees. *It's what's inside that counts,*

Zakkai says, but Federico has fallen
asleep. Zakkai drops the oar overboard.

On dry land, new skin swarms
over the old. Here, the seventy-year-

old place in Zakkai's belly recognizes
only comets. He has never tasted crab.

He has no idea where they are.

Buying a Gun on the Internet, or, I'm Mad at My Family

Three dogs not barking, some kind
of statue, Greek,

their own island sticking, a molar
from blue ocean because

what other color
would it be, here, especially

in this world, a gum swimming
with chill-blooded fish

(their nervous
systems are not

like ours), while Aunt Adelaide

does her morning
meditation. *Kundalini*

before coffee, she always says.
Her eyes dissolve

their sugar, Dravidian
handle-less mug, steaming Caesar,

Caesar steaming at knifepoint—
all over the world, chests open

to laws that demand revising, sodomy
handgun, the threat

of the draft. Aunt
Adelaide defending

her son's penchant for schoolgirls.
After work, he goes

onto the computer, finds why
stupidity is tolerable

in an age of reason, where violence
is only the ocean, driven

by the smallest algae. *If we try,*
we can bioluminesce. Here,

all that is lunar
is debatable.

Situation-specific, Aunt Adelaide says,
warming her river rock

in her palm. *You don't know*
the whole story. This one ends

when the Man in the Moon
drops his pants,

with three dogs not barking,
but squatting in a row, and here

we come in—the first simile,
quadruplicate eyes, such

cubist piles in the lawn—
like cultured flies dying

with the shit.

Sagittarius Nocturne

Night heavy
as a cabbage, and I doze
to the dachshund's
chicken bone vomiting,
then swim, dressed like marriage
in only a cummerbund,
to the wet star on top
of the tool shed, and hear
a single yard of black grass confide
to its finish every morning,
and the coal necklace
on brick where jellyfish,
in blocked uppercase letters,
spell another mystery
without the stroke of a few
fattening photographers,
disorganized white breasts,
the loud treasons of waking.

Shabbat

My aunt screams, *Hak mir nisht ken tshaynik!*
The teakettle in her voice banging
my wife to sleep. A Starling loose
between hip and hair. The white fedora,
as always, stays put on the coattree.

Everyone holds a basket of laundry,
everything washed has its light.
My aunt wonders, why not mother?
frowns at the corncobs, straight
as candles, the brisket, the broth,
the cinnamon,

the two candleflames swimming
in wax, treading water like siblings, all day,
while somewhere in Florida, a broken frog
gives birth to smoke.

Sagittarius Does Syracuse

Foxes seed the city. We light our pipes
with skinny paper; the larger the novel,

the longer the smoke. From the sixteenth
story, you can see Catskills, (long fingernails)

stringing themselves into the sentence
you always use to describe me. *A fantasy*

night-Eden, jade with cats and snake milk.
I pretend the foxes are still alive. I pretend

I know what you're talking about, arms draped
in Sixth Street chintz. When we're reduced

to our gold and our bedposts, our picture frames
and piano keys, I wonder if the ants will

accept you. I wonder if they will build
larger hills from our bones.

Memorial Day

Tonight, we'll have to sleep

in the unsweetened forest

where the birds

lock their wings

and maple

reads like *impale*.

Elegy for the Whitefish

The grandfather, surrounded by Illinois doves,
does not see his wife in the rowboat. She imagines

smothering him in his sleep, his hair pulling off
with the pillowcase. The greenest feather

remembers the earth.

The whitefish dive, their beds behind them.
Women, tighter than glass, forget,

happy...

They raise their fingers before their hands,
whitefish hanging in the seaweed, throat

and spine disown their avenue, begin
to take in air.

Down the street, the synagogue closes its doors,
Rabbi Kaminker packing blue prayer books

into a blue duffel bag. My grandparents can no longer
buy him lunch, but they still remember the pink

of his wrists.

He holds his son to the radiator vent, Mrs. Papier
upstairs singing a Polish opera. In the morning,

he writes my family name on a piece of yellow paper.
He forgets to prepare breakfast,

writing and writing.

Buffalo

With Henry, I am gutting a buffalo.
He says, last week, he fed it fish meal
and black tea. One arrow and a heart
is all it takes to feed us here. Mona
is back from a ceremony in Estonia
with a vicious appetite.

Away from us, alone, my daughter is drawing
a buffalo on the sidewalk. Its face blue, body
pink, eyes as white as paper. I worry when
she steps onto the school bus, and then again
when she comes home.

She is drawing sparks around the animal's head,
I don't know stars or bees, but I bet
on bees. This is summer.

Somewhere, in Estonia or Cleveland,
the queen is still alive, fatherhood
is only a picture.

I gut this buffalo with a stick
of white chalk. This is a faulty tool.
Its stomach opens like a lion's yawn.
Water, warm from an ear, hours
after swimming. I see that it has swallowed
the beehive. This is also a faulty tool.

Sprouts

I like Brussels sprouts. There is something
even about them, as opposed to erratic, as opposed
to odd. Even when alone, they are double. Like
one eye. We see what we're used to.

Architecturally-correct, each is a habitat
with staircases. Typically, I add only gray
salt (from Brittany), and cut it down the middle
with a butter knife. I always expect to find a fly
at its center, looking up at me with red eyes,
indignant that I've halved the work of its mother.

I eat their cores. I think of the brain
and its leaves. At rare times, like after
the Urbana chorus of cellos, or that time
when my brother, Ronald, went through
the windshield, I added the mustard.

The Upstairs Cow

If you lead a cow upstairs, it won't come back down (again:
an intimate fact). Roan, mathematical, its legs plus its stomachs

total eight (a fact for the equivocal heart). In response to this
simple addition, the cow convulses in octets. An errant udder

knocks a post from the railing (like the aorta, a small,
familial detail). She has no choice but to become a rendition

of herself, a spider silkscreened to a purple tie (more, more)...
A spider as white as a calendar's December, a spider that

the father wears, wishing itself a cow, as infinite as a cow
drinking milk (a rare fact: it happened once in Stowe, Vermont).

But this longing is all for the sake of the father. The cow is still
a cow (not a fact). She won't come to the family. To those

downstairs: to the January infant, the cow is rice grains dragging
chainwise over a nursery floor, to the mother,

the cow becomes Jupiter, testing the quality of the fluid in her
(astronomical theory without the equals sign), and to the father,

the tie (plaque in St. Mary's Textile Mill, assistant manager's office).
The three of them gather to a card-table and debate whether the cow

drinks Turkish coffee. The infant has nothing to say on the matter
(the womb becomes an imaginary friend—yet another intimacy, in fact).

Upstairs, the cow lows to the carpet. Downstairs, the father
pretends to come home. The cow is afraid to greet him, but

the father expects her to act like a dog. When she can't, he moves
the family down the stairs indefinitely.

The father tears a kitchen cabinet from its hinges, uses it
as a chalkboard. He writes:

    1)   *The eye of the ostrich is bigger than its brain*
    2)   *Oak trees produce no acorns until the age of 50*
    3)   *Elephants are the only animals that can't jump*

(facts that envy details), and hangs it over his doorbell
as a warning. The family doesn't go so far as to brick

the stairwell over, but their ignoring of the animal allows her
to become the ghost. In this way, the infant is first introduced

to the concept of cellophane (chemical citation, 1919).
The child will wail for a decade. The cow wears no bell

(opinion), nothing rings for her.

Frida Kahlo

When *trova* music becomes too much,
that is real grief. The deck of Tarot

balancing the breakfast table.
The skull card rises

so our eggs won't topple.
This morning, in bed, you

hallucinated an orange grove,
the smell of the pith, and the sour

breath of some insomniac chauffeur.
While waiting for you, you said, he cleans

his teeth with a maraschino stem.
When I shook you: the grief,

the curtains cut to ribbons,
in the courtyard, Maria

massaging the belly of an ox.
Over it, we kiss because we're both

baritones, our fingers rife with oil.
We hide all that is acrylic under

our tongues. You told the band
to leave, forced me to burn the groves,

evict the workers. One of them
will return as the chauffeur, teach us,

poisonously, that our alphabet has no place
in the cruelties of sleep.

1962

I gave birth to this adult sheep
in a square in Valladolid, Mexico.
An old Mayan woman asked
for the wool. I said yes.

The moon folded in like a lung,
knew the ants
were doing it on purpose, lifting
my thighs. Right then, I gave
birth to this adult sheep, couldn't tell
if it was a boy or a girl.
I pushed two ants together,
made them kiss: when they couple
the announcement begins.
Very few are voluptuous,
like a cathedral. Their brittle hips open.

There were six million ants
and a pomelo tree. Only two ants
had energy left to smooth my hair,
cough as they kiss. My mother
wrote a story about it.
I am trying to rewrite it.

I never had a grandfather
on my mother's side. A car accident.
Maximilian. A used car salesman. Once,
took my mother to the circus. Lions.
Once, rigged a doorbell to gently
electrocute. In these ruins,
I had a vision of him. The coat
of the sheep. I said yes. I asked
for good sunlight. Tires
roared and he coughed.
I demand the morning. I sneak
into that car very early. The windshield
is voluptuous as a heart. You coughed
in time with its breaking.

Ossification

You say, art undresses life, shows us its nipples
and suckling pigs, exhumed from palm fronds
and leprosy. You say, it's Easter Island
framed and hung with one gold nail in a beamless
wall. How does it stay up? How can the old man
with one leg not topple when the weather lights

his windbreaker on fire? He claps both hands
over his chest and mutters something about
the hierarchy of clouds. You misinterpret this
as thunder or ash, as the girdle that shapes
the trunk of the plum tree. Pluck one before
the blood shoots to its branches, before its eyes

fill with fluid and spill their quince. Be the giraffe.
I know it's in you. Your mother had it. You bite
one side. I'll bite the other. Meet you at the pit.
If the bomb rings while we're eating, let the machine
get it. At our windowsill, the potted basil attacks
the potted thyme. The winner goes home with the pig.

How dare we deny those whose function is to flavor?
Love reduced to oilpaints. Sex reduced to sculpture.
Remember what Giuseppe said? How Rubens created
his own fetish? He died with a stocking in his mouth.

If you unhook my belt, I'll kiss you. You should
know this: My tongue has gone the way of the wind-
breaker, plum-skin. If you be the giraffe, I'll be
the lioness, open my mouth as an asphodel. Go ahead.

Read me another chapter. Sing me to sleep. And this time,
be specific.

THREE

Aardvark

Letters of Perspective: Father-Daughter

Anatomically, an aardvark belies
its breast, but linguistically,
it rolls its heart down the fucking hill. Think
snowball. How snow allows,

but, baby, beautiful as you are,
never untie the robin, or a flurry
of four mating wings. In the center
of winter, is the bird. In the center
of the bird is not the magic engine
you expect, but a looped recording
of a song called, "You Son of a Bitch."

Called cold, caught in the beak of a very
late night, you will try to revise a moon
for all of us, structure its light
as allegory. You will imagine white
mud at its core, and for blood,
millions of catfish.

Do dragons die like people, you ask
at bedtime. I want to tell you, once,
fire kept us alive. Then, it seemed
revolutionary to name you Dawn.

Eat eleven eels is as insufficient
an incantation as *go fuck yourself*,
bored, ecclesiastic.

Finally, feel. Forgo Maximilian. You never
had a grandfather on your mother's side. A car
salesman in a car accident. Rewrite him
without breaking. As if
tattooing the earth with your tongue.
As if birthing the dragon
from the firefly.

Good God, go to sleep already.
This drinking straight from the milk
carton blues your lips like a corpse.
Open your window. Read the prose
of the traffic. Tell yourself it means
everything in gibberish.

Here, *happy* hovers like tea steam.
Darjeeling or salmonberry. Something
exotic and growing. Something with at least
three syllables. I will have to get used
to this: your waking in wavelengths.
Today: a rattle shaped like a hen.
Tomorrow: in the floral

mucosa of weeds, a hard-on.

Incidentally, insufficient ice
on the windshield, prevents you
from seeing the Buddha of Joliet, Illinois
carving a world of rats from the babblings
of an idiot.

January: jackals jackknife when hit
by a car-ful of Christians. The mother
is the only one who makes it, her hipbone
pushing like a dime, easy, as if
from cotton. The driver frowns, sees
the pups as dead heathens, Bibles
with tight spines. As they drive,
a baby is born in Babylon. A baby
chokes on a moth in Japan.

Kaleidoscopic, Kaisers, Kabuki
worm a warm place for you
at the bottom of the chandelier. They build
you like a fire. In your teens, the tremendous
staircase of iron fists, face-paint,
and myopia will allow you, years later,
to buy a plane ticket. When you make love
for the tenth time, in a pink room overlooking
the Ganges, your fingers clench
like karakul.

Lie listless, like a lobster, knead your hands
into dough. Watch me arrange
your closet, quarter your prom dress
with pinking shears. Don't worry. I'll bring you
a glass of water and a green pill. Surely,
fertility is the claw. The tail, so much like
the brain, obvious with lapse.

Marcos Martinez, molecular biologist,
tells me to tell you, Chile is fat
to a molecule.

Never nullify need. If, in sleep,
you arch your back like a wasp, no one,
but Freud, will notice.

Or, organize: orange with black, red
with green. In color is holiday,
and in holiday, a hammer. Outdo
the neighbors, never come home
alone. Imagine the ocean in your lawn,
the deadbolt, your unceasing oar.

Please: Ponderosa pines or not, the world
is your toothpick. I'm sure you've forgotten
about our camping trips, how your mother
thought the forest looked like matchsticks.
And you: hair standing on end.
For you, fright and spiders
were mutually exclusive. What
can you do, but fish Fire Island
from your molar, Mumbai from the string
of cavities. Allow the botany
and the bluebell to digest their courtship
somewhere behind wisdom. Either way,
the archeologists will unearth
our violent copulations with a shovel
and pail.

Quiet, quiet. Quatrains won't do.
You can't live your life in fours.
Like an animal, or mathematician.

When you were an infant, your uncle
laid feathers at the corners of your crib.
Peregrine falcon. Your mother
told me about his customs, but everything
strangely retarded when, afterward,
he never again blessed
anything of quality.

Really. Rabbis, rack-of-lamb,
and horseradish bless you with permissions.
So you cry. You
and everybody else. Bitter herbs
and *tsimmes* do not a wigwam make. The rabbi
went to Santa Barbara to launch
a congregation for gays and lesbians.
The lamb bought my ticket
to Paris. And, of course, your dream:
The pasturage in Africa. The hollow mare,
ribs like broken bedsprings. You,
with your basket, pouring an icicle
light. But below the light (they must have gotten
too much sun), like hymnals, only four
dead radishes.

So shuck Santiago and eat
her corn. Use the silks for hair
and glasses. Watch for Andromeda,
unhusked in a doorway on the Lower
East Side. In India, find the whale.
But dig slowly, so

try to trivialize the death
of a childhood pet—Ruthie (named
for my mother, the red spot
on her forehead), your goldfish
who you insisted on refrigerating
for 24 hours next to the ladyapples
before burial. You were convinced
she would reemerge from the shoebox
as a bluish whale. It had something
to do with cold. Try. It can't
be done. Like you would say: it is
the booger that, when flicked
with a finger, only sticks
to the thumb.

Understand: ugly people
make you look worse. But only
at breakfast. At night, they will hide
the length of their tongues in your ear.
When they fall, hands joined like the sun,
into your kitchen, look down,
stand under.

Venture, vase-hipped, vanilla under
the tongue, toward the only Bolshevik
orchid the cowboys left standing
in Cheyenne. It will not represent
the organ you think, petaled
with old rain and carpenter ants.
In its pollen, the stench of every bell,
the burning of the world's flags.
When you smell it, thank me.
In our 30s, your mother pushed
for a vasectomy.

Wasp.

X-on xylophone x-pumps drip gasoline
onto your canvas shoes. Filling up,
remember your favorite song
when you were six-years-old.
The one about the owl who nests
in Christmas. The owl knows:
the saguaro is disappearing, one
childish note at a time. Feel our concert
called off like hieroglyphs,
the rubber mallet at the backs
of our knees. Our cancelled music,
you say, zero, once spelled
with an X.

Yesterday, you yelled *yes!*
to the mailman. He didn't realize
you are sick, that your mouth
is a postage stamp, commemorating all bald
honor in sunken warships. I should have
told you. Death is simpler than you think.
Blood is always red. Lust, yellow.

Zeal zips Zimbabwe like a windbreaker.
Zinnias score the sleeves. When I was
your age, it was my first time
in the Southern hemisphere. We marveled
like idiots
at how the toilets swirled backward
when flushed. Marveled at backward.
The property of the tribe.
Your mother burned the pictures
over two cords of alderwood in Alaska,
talked about skins as prisons, feathers
as destined to fail. I must say:
it took the safari for us to realize
that the patterns for all migratory
birds are determined (cooked,
unstriped) in the assholes
of the mythical zebra

with seven legs.

ABOUT THE AUTHOR

Matthew Gavin Frank is the author of the food-and-wine memoir "Barolo" (forthcoming from The University of Nebraska Press), and the poetry chapbooks "Four Hours to Mpumalanga" (Pudding House Publications), and "Aardvark" (West Town Press). Recent work appears in *The New Republic, Field, Epoch, Crazyhorse, Indiana Review, North American Review, Pleiades, The Best Food Writing 2006, The Best Travel Writing 2008 and 2009, Creative Nonfiction, Prairie Schooner, Gastronomica,* and others.

He received the 2005 Summer Fellowship from the Virginia G. Piper Center for Creative Writing, a 2006 Artist's Grant from the Vermont Studio Center, and a 2008 Fellowship in Prose from the Illinois Arts Council.

He was born and raised in Illinois, worked in the restaurant industry for over 15 years, and currently teaches Creative Writing at Grand Valley State University.

Current favorite dessert: Revisionist Caprese Salad: Basil Ice Cream, Buffalo Mozzarella Syrup, Oven-Dried Sweet Tomato, and Tomato Rock Candy.